WEIGHT WATCHER

Fast & Fabulous

COOKBOO

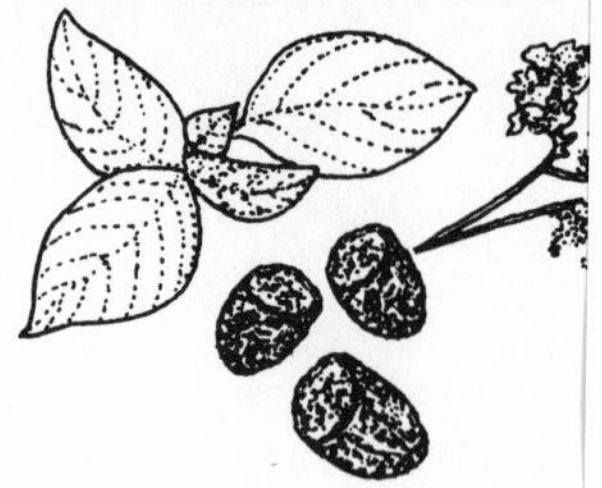